GROWING AS A PROFESSIONAL ARTIST

Business for Breakfast, Volume 10

LEAH CUTTER

Knotted Road Press

Growing Your Inner Artist
Business for Breakfast, Volume 10
Copyright © 2019 Leah Cutter
All rights reserved
Published by Knotted Road Press
www.KnottedRoadPress.com

ISBN: 978-1-64470-014-3

Cover and interior design copyright © 2019 Knotted Road Press
http://www.KnottedRoadPress.com

All rights reserved. Except for brief quotations in critical articles or reviews, the purchaser or reader may not modify, copy, distribute, transmit, display perform, reproduce, publish, license, create derivative works from, transfer or sell any information contained in this book without the express written permission of Leah Cutter or Knotted Road Press. Requests to use or quote this material for any purpose should be addressed to Knotted Road Press.

Disclaimer
This book is provided for general educational purposes. While the author has used her best efforts in preparing this book, Knotted Road Press makes no representation with respect to the accuracy or completeness of the contents, or about the suitability of the information contained herein for any purpose. All content is provided "as is" without warranty of any kind.

Come someplace new…
If you'd like to be notified of new releases, sign up for my newsletter.

I will never spam you or use your email for nefarious purposes. You can also unsubscribe at any time.

http://www.LeahCutter.com/newsletter/

Also by Leah Cutter

The Chronicles of Franklin
Franklin Versus The Popcorn Thief
Franklin Versus The Soul Thief
Franklin Versus The Child Thief

Tanish Empire Trilogy
The Glass Magician
The Desert Heart
The Ghost Dog

The Shadow Wars Trilogy
The Raven and the Dancing Tiger
The Guardian Hound
War Among the Crocodiles

The Clockwork Fairy Kingdom
The Clockwork Fairy Kingdom
The Maker, the Teacher, and the Monster
The Dwarven Wars

Seattle Trolls
The Changeling Troll
The Princess Troll
The Fairy-Bridge Troll

The Cassie Stories
Poisoned Pearls
Tainted Waters
Spoiled Harvest
Bloodied Ice

Contemporary Fantasy

Siren's Call
The Immortals' War
Circle of Air

Contents

Why I'm Writing This Book   vii

Part One
You Are an Artist
Yes, You   3
Introverts   5
Finding Your People   9

Part Two
Recognizing and Dealing With Fear
Fear Messes With Your Head   15
Fear of Failure   21
Fear of Success   23
Imposter Syndrome   27

Part Three
When Life Interferes
Life Rolls   33
Aging Parents and Life Rolls   37
Physical Ailments and Chronic Conditions   41

Part Four
Developing New Attitudes
New Attitudes   49
Finding the Door   53
Building Confidence   57
Honoring Yourself   61

Part Five
This and That
Miscellaneous   67

Refilling the Well	71
Asking for What You Need	73

Part Six
The Professional Side of the Equation

On Being a Professional	77
On Time Every Time	79
Meet Your Deadlines or Communicate	81
Be Prepared	83
Meeting Expectations	85
Valuing Your Work	87
Contracts	89
Work Ethic	91
Check In	93
Read More!	95
About the Author	97
About Knotted Road Press	99

Why I'm Writing This Book

"I want to be you when I grow up."

"You're every woman's hero."

"You represent the avatar of an artist. I want to my own version of you someday."

I hear comments like these a lot, sometimes as often as once a month.

Why do other people feel this way? Why do they express it as such to me?

I figure there are many reasons why. Here are a few:

- I live south of Seattle on six and a half acres of woodlands. The land is beautiful and mostly undeveloped. Yet, civilization is only five minutes away.
- While I adore my husband, and he truly is the love of my life, I don't ever have to live with him. Instead, I built myself a tiny house, separate from the main house, that I live in three to four days a week. It's my art installation, full of wood and warmth.
- I support myself with my fiction and my publishing. I am truly rich, not necessarily in dollars, but in time. I do what I want to do and what I need to do for myself every single day.

Why I'm Writing This Book

- I have self confidence. My husband jokes that I am the Towering Mountain of Confidence. This spills over into many places, such as valuing my work and my art, insisting that I get paid for my work, assuming that I have a place at the table whenever there is business to discuss (never begging), being treated as an equal in all settings.
- I had chronic migraines—between twelve to fifteen per month. I changed my lifestyle and my diet, such that it's been months since my last migraine.

It isn't that I have my shit so together that it no longer stinks. (I have a composting toilet in the tiny house. Trust me. I know how I smell sometimes.) I still make mistakes (huge ones!) I falter. I have chronic health issues, some of which I've overcome, some of which I never will. The chemical balance in my brain isn't always right and things go wonky from time to time, making it difficult to do much of anything. As of fall 2018, I am going through a pretty awful perimenopause, complete with brain fog, night sweats, and inflammation on a monthly basis.

However, I think that this book will help some of you get *your* shit together. (More together.) My husband says that one of my superpowers is "life coaching." I have the ability to say the right thing to the right person at the right time.

Hopefully these are the right words at the right time for you.

I don't know if I would call what I have to say wisdom. That's a loaded term. However, as of this writing, I am in my mid-fifties and I've thought a lot about these things. I do have some experience.

For me, I've always viewed the road to wisdom as a combination of acting, then reflecting, then acting again. Back and forth, always in balance. And that's what my life is right now. Periods of reflection followed by periods of action.

My hope, and yes, the reason why I'm writing this book, is that it will be the right time for you to learn something new, to push past your discomfort and be brave about your art.

One suggestion that I'll make now as well as later, is that if you do find this book helpful, put a reminder in your calendar to revisit the book again in a year's time. Chances are there will be additional things that you learn, or maybe it's just a chance to measure your own growth.

Are you ready?

Leah Cutter
    West of the Mountains
    June 2018

You Are an Artist

Yes, You

My base assumption is that one of the reasons you're reading this book is because you're an artist. (And not just a writer, which many of you are. This is about the greater thing called art.)

But what does that mean?

It means, first and foremost, that you're *different* than most people. There is nothing wrong or shameful about that. I'm aware you've probably heard that before.

Do you actually believe it? Deep in your heart, are you comfortable with being an artist? Are you truly okay with marching to a different drummer?

Or does that fact make you feel ashamed occasionally? Do you question whether or not you're normal? (That is, with the assumption that *normal* is somehow equivalent with *right*. For me and other artists I know, *normal* should be classified as *boring*.)

It isn't always easy to accept that eighty-five to ninety percent of the population *isn't like you*.

Where did I get that number from? Science!

In the mid-80s, scientists conducted an experiment on thousands of people of different ages, different background, different ethnicities, etc.

The experiment went as thus: put a group of people in a quiet, dimly lit room, then play soft music and make everything as comfortable as possible.

After fifteen minutes, when people have gotten really comfortable and relaxed, have the sound of a gunshot go off in the room. Loudly.

Lastly, test people's saliva for traces of adrenaline.

Eighty-five to ninety percent of the people tested no longer had any traces of adrenaline in their saliva after twenty minutes.

Ten to fifteen percent of the people tested still had traces of adrenaline in their saliva for as much as *two hours* after the original gunshot.

Guess who those people were?

You got it. The introverts. (For more information on this study, see *The Highly Sensitive Person* by Elaine N. Aron, Ph. D.)

While I know a few artists who are extroverts—mostly musicians—most artists are introverts.

Different than eighty-five to ninety percent of the population.

Accept your differences. Embrace the fact that you are physically wired differently than everyone else. Keep checking in with yourself when you do feel alienated. Remember that it's okay.

Check In

This is the first of many sections in this book where I'm going to ask you to "check in" with yourself.

What I want you to do is to put the book to the side, close your ereader or turn off your phone or actually put the physical book down and ask yourself a question, or meditate on something.

For this check in, ask yourself this:

Are you okay with being different? How okay are you with this?

As part of growing your inner artist, you need to develop acceptance of your differences. Then either embrace them or forgive yourself for them, depending.

I'll talk more later about not looking outside for judgement but only inside. For now, your work is to accept, embrace, and forgive.

Introverts

I MENTIONED this in the previous section, that most artists are introverts. What does that mean?

The classic definition is that an introvert gets their energy from being alone, while an extrovert gets their energy by being with other people.

For a great infographic on introverts, and dealing with introverts, see the Hamster Ball comic: http://themetapicture.com/how-to-interact-with-the-introverted/. (This infographic literally changed my husband's life. The first time he saw it, he suddenly UNDERSTOOD introversion.)

There are shades of meaning with all of this. There are "social introverts"—that is, introverts who need time with other people though they also need time alone. There are what we refer to as "functional introverts"—that is, an introvert who functions so well in social situations that they frequently fool other people into believing that they're an extrovert, when they actually aren't, and they must have alone time in order to recharge. (I fall into this category.) There are the people who define themselves as "hermits"—those who have a lot of difficulty in social situations, can't make eye contact, need to have something to do rather than talk with other people, etc.

For introverts, the single thing that sucks the most energy out of them are *expectations*.

Going into a social setting (even if it's just with one or two other people) is hard enough. Having to go into a social setting where there are expectations placed on you is exhausting.

For example, suppose that you're going to a friend's party, and this friend is really, really mellow and cool. They know you, accept you as you are, and are okay with you being different. They understand that you may come to their party, sit in the corner and not interact with anyone else, then leave early. They won't pressure you to interact, to "go enjoy yourself", or even do much more than just check in.

If it's a really good friend and they know you well enough, they'll have some task or solitary activity for you to do while you're at the party. It's always easier for an introvert to go to a party if there's something to do other than just talk with people.

Contrast that with something similar to a work function, where you're expected to go and interact. Or you're expected to go and chat up people. Or even if you're expected to go and be responsible for other people. All of that is exhausting.

This brings me to the concept of "non-people." As I've mentioned before, people are exhausting. Getting "peopled out" is a regular thing.

There are, however, "non-people." People whom you can hang out with who are not exhausting. I know a few people who fall into that category for me.

A huge part of what makes them "non-people" is that they have no expectations of me. It's okay if we're just hanging out and reading on our respective corners of the couch.

However, even a non-person can be exhausting after a bit, and you may need some alone time after hanging out with them.

Check In

Where do you fall on the introversion spectrum?

Be honest with yourself. You need to be aware of where you *actually* are, not where other people *want* you to be.

How much time do you need to be around other people?

How much time do you need to be alone?

And it's okay if this time changes depending on the person and the activity.

I am at one extreme when it comes to being an introvert. Remember, I'm a functioning introvert, and I'm able to fool people into thinking I'm an extrovert. (Part of that is because I'm not shy. Being shy and being an introvert are not the same thing.)

For me, I'm happiest if I'm alone eighty percent of the time.

Yup. You read that right. 8-0.

Then, the other twenty percent of the time, I actively *want* to be with people. I enjoy their company.

When I worked at day job, I was the healthiest and happiest if I worked from home. Just being in the office with all those people put so much stress on my body that I'd frequently get sick, even if wasn't something being passed around the office.

Chances are, you aren't at my extreme. Or you may be even more extreme than that.

Figure out what your ratio is. You may or may not ever be able to live your life that way. Or you may find ways in which to do it. (It's one of the reasons why I live in a separate house from my husband three to four days a week. So I don't have to breathe his air. And he's a non-person, for the most part.)

Again, the most important thing here is for you to be honest with yourself about what your needs are. And don't be surprised if they change as you grow more into your artistic self.

Let yourself be different. Let yourself be alone.

Finding Your People

OKAY. So you're different than most of the population. You're starting to acknowledge that, come to an acceptance of that. Embracing it even.

The next step, and this will be an ongoing process, is to find your people.

I don't mean just find people who are okay with your differences. Those friends are invaluable, and you need them as well.

But you also need to find people who are different like you. People you can talk with who will understand your quirks. People who just nod sympathetically when you say, "I'm peopled out," instead of judging you or demanding that you stay just a little while longer at a crowded party.

As an introvert and an artist, it's difficult to find those people. They're kind of in hiding as well.

However, we live in an age where everyone is just across town on the internet, whether or not they're physically there, or in another country.

It will take some work to find your people, the ones who will not only accept you but embrace you and celebrate your differences.

Fortunately, those people are there. You can find them.

Why do you need to find them?

So that you can fully realize that your weirdness is not singular, but shared. So that you have people you can share your heart and passion with. So that you don't feel so alone and isolated all of the time.

I have a young woman who I've been mentoring since she was sixteen. She's now in her mid-twenties. For her twenty-first birthday I took her to a science fiction convention.

For the first time in her life, she was met a large group of people who were *like her*. When she said she was tired and peopled out, instead of getting strange looks, they offered solid advice because they'd all been there. It was a revelation for her, to realize that she was not alone.

Where will you find these people? Meetup.com is one possibility. Another is Facebook. Find groups who do the same thing you like to do, like knit, sew, crochet, write, draw, paint, take photos, bake, grow plants, make models, etc. You may find kindred souls there.

As I said before, it may take you some time to find your people. For growing your inner artist, you need people to support you. Find your people.

Family of Origin, Part One

As you should have expected, I'm going to be talking about family of origin.

Chances are, your family of origin are *not* your people. They may or may not be supportive of your differences.

And this is where you're going to have to do some digging. Serious, possibly painful, digging.

How okay is your family with someone being different? Did they accel at "I'm okay, you're okay"? Or were they always concerned with what someone else was thinking about them? Comparing themselves to their neighbors?

Now, I understand that my family of origin was completely different than most. The ratio of artist to mundane was opposite to what most people experience. There were five of us in my family. Four of the people in the family were introverts as well as creative.

Four of them. Out of five.

I don't think I've ever met any other introvert who grew up in a family like mine. Generally speaking, they might have one other person who had some level of introversion.

The usual ratio would be four people who are extroverts or creatives and only one person (them) would be introverted.

Check In

Yup, this is one of those times when you're going to have to do a serious check in about your family of origin.

While you can get past your family of origin stuff, if you've never done the work before, it's going to take you some time.

So again, put this book to the side, close your eyes, and ask yourself this:

How okay was your family of origin with being different, in general? How okay were they with* you *being different?

The answer may surprise you. Or it may not. It may make you angry. Or sad.

You may need to sit with your feelings for a while as you come to grips with what you grew up with.

Ultimately, you'll need to move past your family of origin and their opinions of your differences. I don't know what you, as an individual, need in order to do that.

You may need to just accept your family as they are. Possibly forgive them. Or in some extreme cases, disown them.

That is part of your individual journey.

What's most important is that you start taking the steps you need to take in order to begin the resolution process.

As I said in the intro, let's go. You can do this.

Recognizing and Dealing With Fear

Fear Messes With Your Head

FEAR IS A POWERFUL MOTIVATOR. It can stop you dead in your tracks, stop you from growing, changing, becoming. Or it can motivate you to even greater feats and heights.

Despite the fact that I am the Towering Mountain I still have fears. Some of them come out of the blue. Some of them are old enemies who I'm used to combatting.

We probably have a few fears in common. You may also have fears that are unique to you, your life and expectations.

I've covered some aspects of fear in <u>The Beginning Professional Writer</u>. I'm going to go deeper into some of the fears that I believe are more universal. As I said in the beginning, the point here is for you to A) Realize that you're not alone, as well as B) Learn some of the techniques I've used to get over those fears.

OMG! You Are Doing It All Wrong

Seriously. The way you are living your life. Pretending to be an *artist*. Wanting time alone. Needing different food than most people. Different clothing. Hell, even your *hairstyle* is wrong.

Does any of that sound familiar? It's part of the "you're an artist" fear.

I believe it's at the base of why most artists are afraid in the first place.

This was why the first chapter was all about accepting the fact that you're an artist. You need to be okay with your differences and just move on.

However, the fear that you're doing everything wrong is huge. It will stop you from accepting yourself. It demands that you compare yourself to others. It allows others' judgement of you to matter, to be important, whether that other be a partner, a parent, a friend, or just society in general.

There are several methods that I use to combat this fear.

—**Familiarization**. One of the things that my husband and I *regularly* say to each other is the title of this subsection. "OMG. We must be doing it all wrong." We poke fun at that saying. A lot. By repeating it out loud so often I've become inured to it. We frequently point out just how we are doing it all wrong as well. As we are both writers, we will comment on our word count, on how much fun we're having, on the style we're using to write (neither of us work from an outline), and so on.

Your art is going to be different. However, this sort of poking fun at a fear takes a lot of the steam out of it.

—**Keep** your eyes on your own work. As I said above, chances are, you're an introvert to some degree.

In addition to getting your energy from time alone, you probably don't do well with external challenges. Most of the introverts I know aren't in competition with other people.

The only person that they like to regularly compete with is themselves.

Though both my husband and I are writers, we don't compete against each other. He's currently writing many more words per day than I am. Yet, he never calls me a slacker, and I don't feel inadequate. Then again, we have different goals when it comes to writing.

Part of the fear of doing it wrong comes from comparing yourself to other people, either their production or their sales.

You need to be aware of just how deadly that is. It's a huge fear that will stop you because you aren't as "success" as that other person.

The only person who gets to judge whether or not you're doing well is you.

That's it.

I'm going to talk more about setting realistic goals later. However, you might want to start thinking about what you can do, just on your own, and not what others can do or how they're doing more than you.

Keep your eyes on your own work. Don't compare yourself to others. Easier said than done, I know, but a goal worth aiming for.

—**Valuing** others' judgement. This one gets trickier for an artist, particularly a commercial artist. The easiest way to measure your "worth" is by tracking the money.

I get it. Money's important. Anyone who says that money isn't important has never had to survive a month on a box of crackers and a jar of peanut butter, or make the decision whether or not to pay the heat or pay for the medications you need.

If you don't feel as though your work isn't good enough to be paid for, well, I'm going to cover that later.

For now, I'm asking you to at least pretend that you're good enough to get paid for the work you do.

And you're not getting paid.

It's a harsh reality for a number of artists. How do you keep going and not let the fear stop you?

Because that's what it is. It's a fear. And it's related to this entire section—that you're doing it wrong because the money isn't pouring in.

I want to broach this another way.

There are things you can control when it comes to being a creative or being an artist.

How other people feel about your work is *not* one of those things. Period.

While sure, I'd like for every single reader to find and adore my writing and demand more, it doesn't work that way.

I cannot control how other people feel about my work. I cannot reach through the ether and control their minds and get them to open their wallets. (If you do have this skill, let me know, maybe we can work out a deal.)

The only thing, the *only* thing, I can control is how often I create the work.

Period.

How many days do I get to the keyboard? How many words do I generate?

For you, it may be different. How many sketches have I drawn this week? How many paintings have I finished? How many squares have I sewn for the latest quilt? How often have I picked up my flute and run scales? How much time have I spent processing photographs?

If you're not a writer, your measure is going to be different than mine. Words are easy to count. You're going to need to sit down and figure out what is a realistic goal for you and your art. It may take you some time to come up with these goals.

Remember, you'll get faster once you develop the habits.

So again, stop letting others outside of you judge the quality of your work.

Instead, show up. Every day. Do the best work you can.

If you're doing that, you're a success and you are, in fact, doing it right.

Period.

Check In

You knew this was coming, right?

I've given you three possible methods for feeling as though you're doing it all wrong.

This check in is a three-parter.

How often do you have the fear that you're doing it all wrong?

Side note: if you're female, you might also want to track whether or not you primarily have this fear only at specific times of the month. For me, I know that I'm most beset by fears the week before my period and much less so the rest of the month.

You may need to sit with this question for a while in order to separate this fear from the others. (As I mentioned earlier, fear is what stops most artists from reaching their full potential. This is merely one of the major fears. There are more that I'll cover later.)

Once you figure out whether or not this fear is a major player in your life, you get to think about the second part of this check in.

I've given you three potential workarounds for this fear. Which, if any, work for you?

If something that I've mentioned above works for you, awesome! You get to move onto the next part. If none of the three I've talked about work for you, you get to sit with this part of the check in for a while and figure out what *will* work for you.

You may need to go back to family of origin materials in order to combat these fears. Maybe it involves arguing in your head with a parent, or possibly parenting your inner child some more. I don't know what you need. I can only offer suggestions and get you thinking about what *you* need in order to deal with this fear.

How are you going to remember this workaround the next time this fear rears its ugly head?

It isn't enough to just recognize the fear and figure out what might work to combat it. You're going to need to start putting those workarounds into practice. What is going to work best for you? Is it sticky notes pasted to your monitor? A sign on the wall of your workspace? A reminder that flashes up now and again on your computer screen, done up as a fancy meme then used as a screensaver? Is it a weekly or monthly calendar reminder, basically an email that you'll get on a regular basis that reminds you of a particular workaround?

Again, I don't know what you need. You're going to have to figure it out for yourself.

This is one of the reasons why I suggest coming back to this book after a year's time. Possibly you figured out a process for yourself, however, after a year's time, you've backslid, or the process no longer works as well. You'll have to come up with a new process so that you can keep growing as an artist and not let these fears hold you back.

Fear of Failure

THE FEAR of failure holds back a lot of artists. They frequently won't even start a new venture because they're afraid they'll fail at it. Sometimes this occurs when just starting a new piece, such as a new novel or a new painting. It often occurs when you're doing something that is a bit new, such as writing in a new genre or working in a new medium.

Do you find it difficult to start new work? It may be a fear of failure that's holding you back.

Do you find it very uncomfortable to change your process? Even if you're aware that your current process isn't healthy? That, too, may be fear of failure holding you back.

Like the "you're doing it wrong" fear, fear of failure often comes about because you're letting other people judge your worth. You're often afraid that *they* won't think that it's good enough or that you're good enough.

Your personal fear of failure may be more nebulous, though. It's a generalized fear, nothing specific.

That should give you a clue on how to fight it…by making the fear specific.

I've talked before (*Beginning Professional Writer*) on what it means to fail. If you haven't done that work, it's one of the things I'd like for you to do right now.

Check In: How do you define failure?

You may need to break this down into more specifics, such as "how do I define failure for this project" versus "what is failure in terms of my career".

One of the things that I emphasized in the previous book was to make sure that you share what you consider failure with your partner. They may or may not have the same fear, or even the same definition.

Once you've defined your failure, take a good hard look at it and determine whether or not the definition involves allowing someone else to judge your work.

For example, if failure for this project means that I don't sell it, guess what? I've allowed something outside of my control to judge the worthiness of a project.

Is your definition of failure that I didn't finish a project? If that's the case, you're going to have to delve deeper into why that project didn't get finished. Was it the wrong project? The wrong time? Did you lose interest? Why? What's holding you back from finishing a project? Is it a project that needs to be finished, or do you need to do something else? Do you never finish projects? Are you afraid of finishing a project (because then other people can judge you…) And so on.

You will probably have to revisit this fear. It will rear its ugly head in myriad forms, particularly after you think you've beaten the beast back.

Fear of Success

SUCCESS ACTUALLY SCARES artists more than failure.
If I fail at something, I know what to do. It's more hard work. More lessons. More practice. More creating.
If I succeed at something…what do I do next?
Fear of success means redefining yourself as a success. You need to change your opinion of yourself. You've finally succeeded! Yay!
What do you do next?
Success is scary. It's a whole new world that you may or may not have encountered before.
The fear of actually succeeding stops more artists than you can imagine. They will frequently stop working on a project as it nears completion because they're afraid that it will succeed.
Fear of success also destroys couples. As I mentioned in Book One (*Beginning Professional Writer*) you must figure out what success means to you, personally, then have a conversation with your partner or spouse or even best-supporting-friend about how *they* define success. Your definitions may end up being wildly different. You need to figure out how to compromise now, before you reach that stage.
Fear of success can be difficult to root out. Partly because, you guessed it, what our definition of success is frequently informed by our family of origin. I know more than one writer who actively sabotaged herself rather than be successful because her family of origin didn't consider her art to be a "real job". (One in particular was

a multiple New York Times bestselling author, who still regularly heard this complaint from her mother.)

How do you deal with fear of success?

First off, you must recognize it when it occurs. Are you stopping before finishing? Are you sabotaging your career when it comes to money? (Many people who weren't raised with money have the mindset that they can never have money, and therefore stop themselves from actually making any.) Do you belittle your art? (Again, do you think you need a "real job"?)

Next comes the tricky part: you need to be okay with being successful.

Remember, success means change. You will have to change your definition of yourself. You will have to become someone new. Someone different. Someone who is a success.

If the thought of that type of change scares you, roots you to your seat with terror, you're probably going to need professional help. It's a big box to unpack on your own. You can do it alone, however, extra help will make the process go faster and more smoothly.

Check In

This one might take some time. Or you might have to come back to it. Possibly this is one of those areas where you set a reminder in your calendar to once a week for a month to sit and think about this.

What is your definition of success?

Your answer must be two-fold.

First, figure out what is your definition of success *that is within your control.* Are you a success because you write every day? Because you paint every weekend? Because you put in so many hours each week processing photos?

This definition may have to vary from project to project.

For example, I'm an indie author. I publish my own writing (as well as the writing of others.) What I term to be a success as a writer is basically getting to the page every day. That's a very different job than being a publisher. Maybe it's coming up with a cover concept this week. Maybe it's formatting three books this week. Or perhaps it's taking a single book all the way through the publishing process in a single week.

You'll note, however, that all of those are completely within my control.

I am a success because I write. A writer writes. Period. Sit down, shut up, write.

What aspect about your art *that you control* defines your success?

Once you have a good grasp on that portion of your process, then and only then should you start giving serious thought to what it means to be a success in terms of things *that are outside of your control*.

This can be a dream as opposed to a goal. (Quick explanation of the difference: a dream is something that would be really nice to have, while a goal is something with actual concrete steps that are in your control that you work toward.)

Winning the lottery is a dream, particularly if you never buy a lottery ticket. It's very far outside your control.

Being able to support yourself through sales of your art is a goal. It takes a lot of steps, and some of it is out of your control. Is that your definition of success? Will you consider yourself a success if you achieve that?

Does your partner or spouse consider that success? Do they have something grander in mind? Or something smaller?

And then the next question—what happens when you achieve that big goal? Do you have goals beyond that?

I know a writer who basically stopped and floundered for half a year when they hit their goal. They had no secondary goal. They didn't know what to do next. They were dreaming too small.

I have lots of dreams as well as goals. May not make them all. Doesn't mean I won't try my hardest regardless.

Imposter Syndrome

THIS IS such a huge fear it's been given a very scientific name. Many very famous people suffer from it. I almost considered giving this fear its own chapter.

Then I thought better of it. I don't want to give any fear such importance.

It's a fear. No more, no less.

Sometimes this fear is tied up with the "OMG you're doing it wrong!" fear, when you're comparing yourself to others and you aren't doing as well as they are, therefore you're an imposter.

The fact that you have *any* success whatsoever should be a good antidote to that.

I will acknowledge that for some people, imposter syndrome is very real. The primary component of this fear is that a person has achieved some level of success through luck, not through their own skill or talent or perseverance or what have you.

Does it take some level of luck to achieve success? I have to admit that I think so.

But.

And this is a very large, in your face, are you listening to me *but*.

No amount of luck will make up for a complete lack of talent.

Period.

Yes, you may have been lucky by getting your work in front of the right people at the right time.

BUT. Those people wouldn't have paid any attention to your work whatsoever if it wasn't good. They would have passed on it.

I know this deep in my bones. Part of that knowledge comes from attending what is called the Anthology Workshop (https://www.deanwesleysmith.com/workshops/) for years. As part of the workshop, the participants get to sit and watch the six to seven editors at the front of the room explain why they think the current story being commented either works or doesn't. And they do this for every single story in the workshop, all 250 of them.

I cannot tell you the number of times I've watched the editors who are *not* the purchasing editor all rave about a particular story, how good that story is, how perfectly it fits the theme, only to watch the purchasing editor turn the story down, either because they already have a similar story, or it doesn't fit the anthology, or it just didn't catch them.

Selling those short stories was luck to some extent—getting your story in front of the right editor at the right time.

However, if the work *wasn't good enough* it would never sell to an editor. Any editor. Period.

Check In

Do you have imposter syndrome?

If not, great! Skip this. Move on to the next section.

If you do have imposter syndrome, read on.

I don't have imposter syndrome. Then again, I have both my internal definition of success (that I write) as well as my external, long-term definitions of success (making truly stupid amounts of money from my writing).

However, there was a time in my life where I was being told on a regular basis that the *only* reason I was selling fiction was because I was lucky. (I'll talk more about making painful cuts later.) It was bullshit then and it remains bullshit. The only reason I never fell completely into imposter syndrome was because I'm too stubborn. (And yes, more about being a contrarian later as well.)

So take a deep breath, put this book to one side and ask yourself all of the following questions.

Why do you feel as though you're an imposter?
Is it because you're comparing yourself to others? Do you feel your success, which is lesser, makes you an imposter?

If so, you need to look behind you. Where were you a month ago? Six months ago? A year ago?

Look at the reality of the situation. There are people who are ahead of you on the road. There always will be.

There are also people behind you on the road, people who do not have your level of success. Are they imposters too?

Look at where you are. The only way you got there was through talent and work.

Do you feel as though you're successful merely due to luck?
This is where you're going to have to start unpacking stuff.

Is your imposter syndrome caused by family of origin beliefs?
Did they think that the only way one got ahead was through connections, being born wealthy, through being lucky, etc.?

You're going to need to sit and think about that question for a long while. And you might not ever be able to completely get over it. This is where professional help kicks in, because you will need to come up with workarounds so that you continue to be successful and grow as an artist despite feeling like an imposter. (I know of more than one writer who struggles with this. However, they no longer let this fear get in the way or stop them.) And that's the goal here—to keep moving and growing as an artist regardless of a fear.

The other hard question you're going to need to ask yourself is this:

Is there anyone currently in your life who is contributing to your feeling of being an imposter?

If the answer to this one is yes, you're going to have to spend sometime figuring out what to do. If it's a friend, you may be able to easily cut them out of your life.

If it's a spouse, a partner, or a loved one, it's going to be a lot more messy.

Can you get them to change their mind? Doubtful. Remember how scared you may have been when I asked you about becoming someone new and allowing yourself to be a success? It's going to be just as difficult for them to change as well.

Changing yourself to become someone new is one of the most rewarding things possible.

It's also one of the most difficult if you aren't used to it.

Asking someone else to change means you're asking for a tremendous amount of work on their part. They may or may not want to do it. Chances are, they won't.

So this check in might end up being long and difficult and you may end up in a completely different place than where you started.

That's okay. You can do this.

Let's go.

When Life Interferes

Life Rolls

THERE ARE times when life is just going to get in the way of being an artist. There's no getting away from this. Possibly if you lived as a hermit up on the top of a mountain and had a faithful following who brought you everything you needed so you never had any extremal interference...

But I don't really know anyone who's achieved that. The rest of us live in a messy reality.

There are several ways in which life is going to regularly interfere with your art.

The first, and most important, is your family.

Children

If you have children, I'm sorry, but they must come first. They are going to be small for such a short amount of time. They need you. And they are worthy of your full, undivided attention.

The art will still be there. Trust me on this one. It may take you a while to delve back into it. The years you've spent with your kids won't be wasted. Instead, spend them deepening the well of your creativity. You'll be able to bring a new maturity to your art. Or possibly, if you've learned anything from your kids, a new playfulness.

If you're an artist, you will still commit art even when the kids are small, even if you only have five minutes a day, even if you need to redefine your art for a short period of time (such as making sure that not only is there dinner on the table every day, but that it looks gorgeous.)

(Side note, remember what I said before about how exhausting expectations are? Even though you may feel as though you're not doing much, all those demands are going to drain you. Be gentle and patient with yourself.)

There are people I know who, as far as I'm concerned, have managed the impossible, that is, regularly creating their art with small children in the house. There's one writer who was able to write every day, but only for fifteen to twenty minutes, when her two boys had laid down for their nap in the afternoon. There's another writer I know who managed to complete her novels despite the fact that she only had five minutes per day to write.

Seriously. These women are my heroes. I am in awe of their discipline and their drive and how much they want it.

There are other artists I know who put the art aside until the children have gone to school. That's okay too. Don't beat yourself up if that's the type of artist you are. I'm not sure that I could have continue writing if I'd had kids. Quite frankly, it's one of the reasons why I never did. (I knew I didn't want kids when I was a teenager, and I never changed my mind.)

So if you have kids, you need to be gentle with yourself when it comes to the art. Do what you can when they're sleeping or at school. You cannot shortchange them. You cannot strictly focus on your art. Your kids need you. You've made a commitment to them by having them. Keep it.

Check In

If you don't have kids, skip this.

If you have kids, this is a short check in.

Are you resentful of the time you spend with your children away from your art?

I suspect that the answer is, "Duh."

You'll need to do some of this work now, but more in the future.

Do not let this resentment slow you down once you do have time. It's a common enough line from an overly-dramatic movie. "I gave you the best years of my life…"

Do not let that become *your* life.

Cherish the time you've spent with your kids. Know that you've done your best. And as I've mentioned above, realize that when you do get back to your art, you'll have both a better understanding of it as well as a deeper appreciation for it.

Aging Parents and Life Rolls

AT SOME POINT, either your parents, parent-like figures, or even mentors, are going to grow old and die on you.

Shocking, I know, right?

If you become the primary caregiver for an aging relative or mentor, it will interfere with your art. It might not happen while they're in the hospital—your art may become how you deal with all of that. (I've known a couple of artists for whom that was the case.) Just don't be surprised if afterward, when your life calms down again, you suddenly find yourself unable to produce.

Death will interfere with your art. It just happens that way.

It may take you days to process. Or weeks. Or months. Occasionally it will take years, depending. (I know one writer who cared for a diminished parent for over a decade. While she got back to the writing fairly quickly, it did take her over a year to fully recover. But she'd also spent years in a bad place.)

Among my group of friends, we call that a "life roll." It's a roll of the dice, nothing you can predict or necessarily even prepare for, that sweeps your art away from you for a while.

These are the times when you need to be gentle with yourself.

You may or may not be able to produce while caretaking. It's really going to depend on your situation.

Again, be gentle with yourself.

The art will still be there.

How do you know when the life roll is finished?

Not when you start producing again. I know many of you are surprised that isn't the answer.

No, the answer is when you can consistently stay standing, feeling as though your head's above water.

Grief hits us in waves. You're going to be fine for a day, a week, a month. Then you're going to be bowled over again like a wave on the beach and have to drag yourself back up out of that hole.

Life rolls frequently take a lot of time to overcome completely. And you may not ever get over your grief. It will mellow in time but you may still have down days.

And one more time—be gentle with yourself. Forgive yourself for having feelings and flaws. Move on when you can.

For me, when I had a series of life rolls (including but not limited to the death of my mother, losing my job, getting divorced, moving between states and leaving my kitty behind, all of which occurred in a six month period), I stopped writing for a couple of years. I did other art. I sketched, I painted watercolors, I made quilts, I knit. There just weren't many words.

Eventually, I knew that it was time to get back to writing. I started out by using *A Writer's Book of Days* by Judy Reeves. This book contains a writing prompt for every day of the year. I started doing a timed prompt every day to prime the pump. I finally had a writing prompt that not only started me writing again, but quickly turned into a sprawling trilogy.

Check In

This is a fairly simple check in that hopefully most of you will be able to skip. But for some of you, I need to ask this question:

If you're currently struggling with your art, could it be because you're still going through a life roll?

I had a friend who was bitching because creating art had become a chore. I had to point out to him that he'd had a series of life rolls that had all accumulated: his wife had just retired and they were adjusting to a new schedule, he'd changed offices and computers and wasn't comfortable with the new setup, they'd just lost a dear feline companion, and his brother had recently died (they weren't close).

None of those had been enough to completely derail him. Added up together though, they'd thrown him under the water. He needed to take some time off, refill the well, play with his granddaughter, do some gardening. He paused until he couldn't wait to get back to the drawing board, which took about a month. About a week before he started back up again, he would wake up with thoughts of drawing again, though nothing drew him to the sketch pad until he finally had an image he couldn't let go of.

Physical Ailments and Chronic Conditions

I AM a lot (a *lot*) healthier than I used to be. I no longer have chronic migraines.

I still get sick. Just this last week I lost two days of production due to a stomach flu. (Ugh.)

In addition to that, I have issues with my hormones. I will lose days of work each month due to those. For example, there will be nights when I can't sleep due to hormonal fluctuations. (Night sweats are no fun. Nor are the occasional panic attacks that are brought on by hormones alone.) The day after one of these sleepless nights, there isn't enough caffeine in the entire world to get me properly awake. I will get to the page, but I may not be able to produce much.

If you get sick, your first priority is to get well. Period. Do what you need to do in order to get yourself healthy, even if that means not producing for a day or a week.

I know that's difficult to hear as well as to do. My husband gives me grief all the time about working despite being sick.

What he doesn't understand is that for the longest time I *had* to work while I was sick. If I only worked while I was well, I wouldn't work at all.

I have a great fear that all my health will vanish overnight at some point. That I'll suddenly be back to where I was. This is a motivational fear to do as much as I can every day that I can, not a fear that stops me from producing.

So this is going to be a case of do what I say, not necessarily what I do.

If you're sick with a one-time thing, be gentle with yourself and only work if you can.

Another example of this is exhaustion. My husband and I recently replaced the roof on the pump house (that holds the pump and water tank for the well on the farm.) We removed all the shingles one day, replaced half the roof deck on the next day, took a day off, replaced the other half of the roof deck, then spent a day putting on the tar paper and shingles.

We worked too long on that last day, pushing to get the job done. It didn't help matters that we were in the middle of a heat wave and it was ninety-five degrees outside.

Despite wanting to write, to make my daily word count, there just weren't any words for two days. I was exhausted and I needed to recover.

By the third day, I was able to work again. But I had to remember to be gentle with myself in the meanwhile, because I just couldn't work.

There is another side of this: what to do if you have a chronic condition, such as migraines or hormones or something else that regularly takes you out.

Your answer to that is going to be specifically up to you.

My only advice is that you not stay there, wherever that condition takes you.

You remember when I asked about changing yourself in a previous chapter? Becoming someone new if you became a success?

In order to get healthy from a chronic condition, you must believe that you *can* get better. You can heal. Or you can change your life such that you'll be able to mitigate your symptoms.

One of the things that I specifically did when I had such horrible migraines was completely change my diet. I started following the Wahls' Protocol (https://terrywahls.com/).

The Wahls' protocol was developed by Dr. Terry Wahls to help her overcome her multiple sclerosis (MS).

This may or may not sound weird to you. However, by following the diet specified by Dr. Wahls, people are *curing* their MS.

Yes, you read that right.

If a person is young, and if that person goes on the diet when they're first diagnosed, and that person never takes the MS drugs, there have been many reports of their MS symptoms disappearing. Including the lesions that a patient gets on their spinal cord and in their brain.

Do I think that all chronic conditions are caused by diet? No. I know better than that.

Do I believe that a lot more chronic conditions than Western medicine realizes are caused by diet? Absolutely.

For example, I used to get sinus infections all the damned time. Three, four, possibly five every year. I was constantly sneezing and sniffling. I lived on antihistamines. I frequently lost days due to allergy attacks.

Turned out that I *wasn't* actually allergic to everything green and growing, as well as mold and dust.

Instead, I was allergic to the food I was eating. Once I got rid of all grain as well as the sugar, the majority of my symptom vanished.

If you are suffering like I was with horrible allergies all the time and frequent sinus issues or ear infections, you might want to take a good hard look at your diet. Change things up.

For me, going gluten free did nothing. I had to be **grain** free to get relief.

That being said, I still have hormone issues that take me out on a predictable basis. Because I have a healthy diet, I generally only lose two to three days a month.

On those days, I have much lower expectations of myself. At this time, my goal is to write 4000 words every day. However, when I'm not feeling well, I get to write 500 words. That's it.

You may or may not be able to produce on the days when your chronic condition takes you out. Only you are going to be able to judge that. Perhaps those are the days when you consume art instead of produce it, for example, reading books or visiting art galleries online.

As for me and my chronic condition, the good news is that I've reduced the number of days when I can't work to very few.

The bad news is that at this point, I'm not sure I can completely get rid of all my symptoms.

And the other news, that's just news and shouldn't come as a shock to anyone, I'm too stubborn to give up. So I keep trying new and different things, making tweaks to my diet, so that I might get rid of all my hormone issues.

Stay tuned.

Check In

This check in may piss you off. That's okay. You can yell at me all you want. Send me hate mail. I'm not going to take it personally.

However, you need to ask yourself this:

How much of your identity is tied up in being unhealthy?

There are people I know who *will not* work on getting healthy or being healthy, who will not even take the first step toward health, because that would mean change. They are too committed to being sick. It allows them to make all sorts of excuses for their behavior, for not trying new things, for staying at home.

I know that change is difficult. I understand that it's one of the hardest things you may ever try to do. Plus, there's no guarantee that you'll be successful if you change, that is, completely well.

However, I maintain that being sick is worse. And until you try, really truly try something new, you'll never know if it actually was possible for you to get well.

Again, how much of your self-identity is tied up with being sick?

You may need to change your definition of what healthy looks like as well. That happened to me when I was finally diagnosed with a thyroid condition. (Side note: I had a hypothyroid condition for decades. You know, the one that makes you exhausted and causes you to gain weight. I refused to stop, and so drove myself into complete exhaustion regularly. Yes, I am that stubborn.)

Before, I was diagnosed, I had only taken medication when I was sick.

Now, I had to take medication every day. Even though at that point I was well and no longer feeling sick.

To stay healthy, I have to take pills every day. And I had to redefine myself as someone who is healthy and takes medication regularly. I cannot maintain a healthy chemical balance without medication.

You may need to do the same, thinking about your definition of what healthy means and keeping it accurate for yourself and your condition.

Developing New Attitudes

New Attitudes

I'VE COVERED a lot of things that may be holding you back from growing as an artist. The fears, the life rolls, and so on.

As you start to address those, you need to also start thinking about the next steps, what else you can do to grow your inner artist. This is going to involve changing the attitude you may have regarding other people as well as your art.

Contrarian

I was born a natural contrarian. I'm pretty sure I can blame part of it on being an artist, as most of the artists that I know have some level of contrariness. (Again, this goes back to being different than most of the people around you. You build up some resistance and push back when you're in that situation.)

If someone tells me that I can't do something, my automatic first response is frequently, "Fuck you." That's just part of my nature.

As an artist, you need to develop some level of this response. It doesn't have to be as harsh. It still needs to be as automatic.

Why?

As a contrarian, I question things. As an artist, so should you. It also means not accepting the status quo. Not all art is comfortable. It also means not accepting the limitations that other people place on me. Or that I may place on myself.

It's a natural defense mechanism. Particularly when it comes to a society that wants you to "behave" and "stay in line" and "be quiet".

That's not what artists do.

I'm not saying that you need to automatically respond with a negative every time you're faced with a limitation.

I am saying that you need to look at those limitations and consciously decide if they make sense for you.

Again, for some of you, this is advanced work, pushing your boundaries. For many of you, you're already in this zone.

Check In

This was actually a difficult check in to write. Not because I didn't think it was important, but because it's difficult to strike a balance.

That gave me the key here to what I should ask.

Do you have a healthy balance between pushing back and accepting?

I would suspect that a lot of you don't have a healthy balance. You accept, and accept, and accept, until you explode and start saying, "fuck you" to everything and everyone.

I've talked before about the difference between the inner creative voice (best represented by a two year old who wants to take off all their clothes and to run around naked outside) and the critical voice (best represented by the parent who is trying to keep you safe).

Your inner contrarian is your two year old. You need to strike a bargain with them. Give in and play, let them run around naked, go have fun for a while. Trust that your creative voice knows what it's doing when it says, "NO!" You might find it testing its limits to start with, but I think with time and patience, you will be able to strike a balance.

Or you may find that you need to say "no" to external things more often, or to your critical voice. If that's the case, this is where a lot of personal growth is going to start taking place.

I know that society will try to define you as "selfish" for taking time on your own, for being by yourself, for staring out a window and making shit up.

Fuck them.

Which is hard for some of you to say. I'm going to get more into developing your sense of self-worth later.

This is also where I go back to the first, basic premise of this book.

You are an artist. You are physically wired differently than eighty-five to ninety percent of the population.

What society considers "normal" is not for you. It will not fit you. You need to develop your own inner contrarian so that you will be able to do what is normal *for you*.

Let me repeat that.

You need to figure out what is normal *for you*.

Then you're going to need to figure out how to achieve that. And part of that work is going to be developing your own inner contrarian.

There's no getting around it. You're going to need to have the ability to push back. Or else you won't be able to grow as an artist.

It's that important.

Finding the Door

I'M ASSUMING that as an artist, you've already started to figure out your path.

However, if you're blocked or having difficulty with the path you've chosen, I want you to consider the possibility that you're on the wrong path.

It may be that you're going through a life roll and haven't recovered yet. It took me two years to recover from all the losses I experienced in a very short period of time. Please take that into consideration.

However, it may be that you need to find a different way.

More than one of the artists I know and have worked with didn't even understand that there was a door standing in front of them. They were stuck and didn't know how to proceed.

What you'll need to do in this case is to find someone who is further along the path than you. It doesn't matter what art it is that they do. You will be able to translate whatever advice they give you into your field. (For example, I know several authors who watch the TV show *The Voice*. The advice that the experts give to their singers is applicable to all arts.)

But find that person or people or group. Not people who just talk about their art—you can find those people damned near everywhere. Don't deal with wannabes or who we refer to as "junior varsity"—

those who talk a lot but do little, or have done very little in their field.

You need to find people who are actually *creating*. Who regularly commit art. Who have been doing it for a while. Who are professionals in their attitude. Who have a work ethic and consistently produce.

Talk with them about their art. (Trust me, even hard-core introverts are delighted to talk about their art.) Ask about their creative process. Ask about their production.

See if they can help you identify that door that's currently slammed shut in front of you.

Once you find that door, once you develop the vocabulary and motivation and possibly healing that you need, go and kick it in.

You can do it. It may seem insurmountable at first. But you're an artist. You've been developing your inner contrarian, having regular drinks after dinner with them, listening to them curse and rant.

Don't let that door block your full potential.

Find that door.

Kick the fucker in.

My husband and I talk with a lot of artists. We try to show people the door on a regular basis.

What astonishes me is how few actually go ahead and kick the damned door in. Most stay on this side of it and continue to complain. They're too afraid of change.

The few who do walk through the door are worth their weight in gold.

So if you're having issues growing your inner artist, you may want to think about whether or not you have a door that's blocking you, hiding your eventual path.

And kick it in.

Check In

I'm not going to ask about being blocked. What I am going to ask is for you to think about the artists who are in your life, as well as those who you are listening to.

Who is giving you advice?

Who do you listen to when it comes to growing your art? Remember at the beginning I asked you to find your people. Hopefully you've already done that. You have people who are artists who you can talk with regarding your art.

Since we are concerned with growing your inner artist, I want to make sure that you're listening to the right people.

There are so many wannabes. People who talk about their art without ever actually doing it.

You may or may not want these people in your life. Just know that the people who are not committing art are likely to be jealous of you and may be trying to stop you, whether they realize it or not.

I have written a lot. For many, many years. At this point, I've completed over thirty novels. While I'm sure that I can learn something from someone who has only written three novels, chances are, it's just tidbits.

Instead, I'm looking for people who have long careers, who have written for decades, who have written more novels than I have.

Chances are, the advice they give me will be more inline with what I need to learn.

That isn't to say that I don't question (or even frequently disagree!) with the people I consider my mentors. I treat them with respect and I don't call them out in public. That isn't my place.

And though I've had some wonderful mentors over the past decade, I still go looking for other voices, other people to listen to. One of the things that I've learned over and over again—while my mentors may say X, some people will never hear it. Someone else may say X with a different accent, using different words, and suddenly a lightbulb will go off.

This is why I'm reiterating that you may want to review this book again in a year or so. It isn't that the words will have changed. But hopefully, you will have. You will be in a different place. You may or may not get a completely different message the second time around.

Building Confidence

As I've stated before, I have a lot of self confidence. I probably always have. Part of that came from having a father who told me I could do anything and who treated me like my two brothers. As a kid, that pissed me off, because it meant that not only did I have to do all the "boy" type work, like shoveling snow and changing the oil in the cars, it meant I also had to do all the "girl" type work like washing dishes and cleaning bathrooms.

It wasn't until I was older that I came to realize that my father also cleaned the bathrooms and washed the kitchen floor at least once a month. Eventually I truly appreciated the fact that he taught me how to fix everything and to do things, like repairing a toilet or rewiring a light switch.

Being taught that sort of thing as a child really helped develop my confidence. There were so many things that I could do. I didn't have to be good at all of them, but I knew how to learn and figure things out.

Most artists didn't have that growing up. Instead, they were mocked for being different, punished for not fitting in, etc.

One thing to note—in my twenties I had a lot of that confidence knocked out of me. I was in a bad situation, being gaslighted. (Original definition of the word includes being manipulated so as to question your own sanity. The word is more generalized now, to include someone questioning your abilities so often that you start to doubt yourself.)

Once I realized what was happening to me, I started doing what I call *reality checks*. I would take long walks in the evening and compare what was being said to me versus what the actual reality of the situation was.

Those reality checks really helped me regain my belief in myself. I was doing the right thing and just being told that I wasn't.

It still took years for me to regain my self-confidence, to get myself back to the point where I marched to my own drummer and I didn't care what society or those around me thought.

I went traveling for a few years outside the United States. After about a year and a half of successfully traveling by myself, after having found work in England, Hungary, and Taiwan, after having negotiated all sorts of different countries and cultures, there was something inside me that was still convinced that *I was doing it all wrong*.

I will never forget the day on the beach in Taiwan where I talked to myself and did a hard-core reality check, comparing where I actually was and what I'd actually done versus those really loud voices in my head.

I finally came to the realization that I was *not*, in fact, doing it all wrong. Instead, I was traveling how *I* needed to travel, doing what was right for me and for no one else.

For example, I tended to travel to fewer places than the other travelers I met. I would land in a city and generally spend three to four days there before moving on. I visited fewer places than most travelers.

What I was doing that they were no doing was two fold. One, I generally tried to write a new short story in every city I visited, and that would take a few days. Two, I would get way off the beaten path and go explore the parts of the city that were generally only seen by natives. I had wonderful experiences that way, rich and deep and that I still remember.

But because I'd missed so many sites and places, I was obviously *doing it all wrong*.

Fuck that.

For building your own self confidence, I would suggest starting with some reality checks.

And by that, I mean looking at what you have *actually* achieved, not with what society expects you to have done at this point in your life, or your parents. There is no comparison with others in a reality check. You can't think about what your high school buddies have achieved and compare it to yourself. You can only think about what is real and in front of you. No judgement is allowed.

What have you achieved? I bet it's more than you realize.

It may be very difficult for you to look at your actual, real life. That's okay. You may need to do this in several phases, baby steps. Maybe just look at what's in front of you today and not look back. Get comfortable with what's really there today and today only. And after doing that for a week start looking back.

There are other things you can do to help build more confidence.

First, I want to reiterate that as an artist, you're different than most people.

Some people are going to find those differences threatening. They will dismiss you out of hand. They don't want to hear from you.

And you know my response to that. Fuck 'em.

But other people are going to find you absolutely fascinating. You have a different way of looking at the world, of thinking about the world. You are one of the most interesting people they know.

And that reality is something else that you can use to help build your self confidence. It's one of the things that I always told myself before I went into a new social situation: I am an interesting person, with interesting things to talk about.

Let me repeat that—*You* are an interesting person (artist) with interesting things to talk about.

So let yourself be interesting, excited about your art and the stuff you've learned recently. You'll find people to geek out with.

On some occasions, you won't. You can leave those early.

Check In

Pretty obvious what this check in is going to be about…
What is the reality of your achievements?

Again, no comparison here. No judgement. Just a straightforward review of what you are doing, have been doing, are capable of doing. Period.

You can't start thinking about all the things you haven't done at this point. Or the things you should have done.

Nope.

The only thing, *the only thing* to think about with this check in is what you have achieved. The actual things.

If this is extremely difficult for you, you may need to start doing more reality checks on what is actually occurring in front of you. Don't let yourself drift away or not be present. Be in the reality of the situation.

This may take a lot of time. But you will get used to it, and be capable of staying in the moment, in the reality of the situation.

You cannot change what's going on until you actually see it. It's that simple.

Honoring Yourself

THIS PART really goes hand in hand with the previous section, about building your self confidence. However, it's enough different that I felt it needed its own section.

This isn't just about honoring yourself. You also need to honor your work.

As an artist, you must be able to value your work. I don't mean in an egotistical *ain't I the best*, but with healthy pride.

There is such a thing as pride that is healthy, BTW. If you've never seen it, you need to go talk with more artists, people who are real artists. Not every artist is self-effacing and believes that everything they do is crap.

For the most part, a healthy artist likes their work. Sure, they'll always be able to find things to critique about it, but deep down, they'll like it. Or they'll like some aspect of it.

I know two artists in particular who firmly, deeply believe that everything they produce is crap. They've both been through therapy and realize that belief system came from their family of origin. They produce and continue to grow as artists regardless. But that's a lot of hard work and some pretty hardcore coping mechanisms.

If it's possible for you, it's much easier to just admit that you're a good artist, that you're good at whatever art it is that you do.

I understand that society frowns on you claiming pride in your work. You should also know by now my opinion of someone external to me telling me how I should feel about something I've produced. (You got it. Fuck 'em.)

I am proud of the books and stories I've written and published. I know I'm a good writer as well as a good storyteller.

Does this mean I can never get better? Heck no. There's always more to learn, more growing for me to do. It's one of the joys about the arts—there's always more to learn, always something new to strive for. I'll never get bored as a writer, not as long as I'm constantly learning.

You need to be able to say that about your own work.

Why?

Because we're talking about growing your inner artist here.

The other side of the coin of knowing that you're good is knowing what you're good at. Me, I get reviews from complete strangers bitching at me because it was 2:00 in the morning and they couldn't put the book down. (Seriously. I've had a couple of these.) So I know that I write page-turning books. In addition, I frequently get told that a reader has never read anything like what I've written, that I'm wildly creative. (Yes, those words exactly appear in more than one review.)

So I know I'm good, I know what I'm good at.

This means I get to practice the other things, like cliffhangers and dialogue and setting and Voice. Every novel I practice something new so I can get better and better.

If you honestly believe that everything you create is crap, how can you get better? Plus, how will you know what to practice if it's all the same crap?

Your inner artist is that two year old who just wants to play. If you constantly tell her that she'd no good, that what she produces is no good, guess what? She may go pout in the corner and not want to come out and play again.

In addition, honoring your work means believing—insisting—that you deserve to be paid a fair price for your work.

The old tired refrain that "information wants to be free" doesn't apply to you, the artist. You provide *entertainment,* not merely information. And as a society we have always, always paid for our entertainment. Look at how much we pay celebrities, whether they be actors, singers, professional sports people.

I know in my particular art, the written word, that sometimes price is driven by the marketplace. For example, romance novels tend to be less expensive, while mystery novels and thrillers tend to be more expensive. I also know romance writers who charge a premium for their work, and their readers happily pay the price they ask.

Value your work.

Check In

This one is really simple.

Do you value the art you create?

Remember, you are a unique individual with a unique perspective. You are an artist. Therefore, the work you create is of value, for no other reason than that.

There needs to be more art in the world.

Be proud of what you do.

This and That

Miscellaneous

WHEN I FIRST STARTED THINKING ABOUT writing this book, I was on a long drive with my husband. We started brain storming all the chapters and sections. I took notes, and have strung together most of the topics we brought up. This chapter is not as coherent, but I still wanted to have these sections in the book.

Twenty Second of Courage

I did not come up with this concept. It came from one of my favorite fitness sites, Nerd Fitness (https://www.nerdfitness.com/blog/the-20-second-challenge/).

The basic concept is this: You don't have to be brave all the time.

All I'm asking from you, is that for twenty seconds, be or do or try something that scares you.

That's it.

You don't have to be brave all the time. That's too big of a change for some of you. Life's already scary and hard. I get that.

But surely you can be brave for twenty second?

If whatever you try doesn't work, you'll become more resilient because guess what? The world did *not* end when you tried something new.

If it does work, woo hoo! You've conquered something and become someone new! That's kinda awesome, and you know that.

You do NOT have to use it all the time. Start off small and slow, say, once a week. Put a reminder every day in your calendar so you'll remember to use your twenty seconds.

But do use it at least once a week. Take twenty seconds and be brave. Be courageous. Be different.

Be the most complete you that you can be.

Starting with only twenty seconds at a time.

You can do this.

Here's the link to the full article again:

https://www.nerdfitness.com/blog/the-20-second-challenge/

Making the Painful Cuts

I realize that I'm unusual when it comes to choosing to write fiction. I knew before I was eight years old that I wanted to become a writer. (I wrote it down first when I was eight, that when I grew up I wanted to be a writer. But I'd always had that dream. I honestly don't remember a time when I didn't want to be a writer.)

Sometime in my late teens or early twenties I learned that I wrote best when I was happy. The idea that I needed to suffer for my art was total bullshit. Living in an attic and starving myself would lead me to produce crap. I produced the best work when I was happy. Period.

These two things led me to make changes when I needed to. The writing was important, and so was my happiness.

As I grew older and I was able to prioritize the writing more, I found myself doing regular evaluations of my life. I started asking myself, "Does this support the writing?"

If so, great! Let's keep doing it.

If this doesn't support the writing, then why am I doing this activity?

I also, sometime in my thirties, started asking this question of the people around me. "Does this person support the writing?"

If so, keep them close.

If not, move them out to an outer circle, demote them from friend to acquaintance.

I cannot tell you the number of times I had to make these decisions.

But because I honored myself and my writing, I knew they were right. They weren't necessarily easy decisions. Sometimes I feel melancholy about the people I've left behind. However, I have no doubt that I made the right choice.

My husband has done the same thing, though under different circumstances. One of the things that his mother told him that he's always remembered is: "It's okay to outgrow your friends."

I know that's going to be harsh for some of you. It's also the truth.

You are sometimes going to have to make painful cuts in order for you to be a better, more complete artist. They won't necessarily be easy, but afterward, your inner artist will let you know you did the right thing by the lack of stress and sudden relief you feel.

This comes to activities as well. I don't have a TV. I do watch TV occasionally on my computer. Basically, I have a rotating list of shows that I watch over the course of a year, and so I end up watching roughly a single episode of a single show once a week. I also listen to podcasts, usually when I'm gardening or cleaning or something.

I don't play video games. I do work out, but I've always found that the more my body is moving, the more the words are flowing. Time in the gym (or working out at the farm) supports the writing, so it's an activity I keep.

I hang out with different groups of friends on a regular basis. I also spend time with other art. Those fill the well instead of draining it. But if any of that got to be too much, I would cut it. The writing is too important.

Check In

You knew this one was coming.

Do the people around you support your art?

The answer may be complicated if you're talking about a spouse, particularly one who provides most of the income for your family.

I can't give you an easy solution for this. It's something you may need to sit with for a long while. You may need to spend a lot of time communicating with your spouse about your needs, getting them to understand that you're different and that's okay, getting them to respect your art even if it isn't bringing in a lot of income at the time.

I do not envy you your journey. Depending on your relationship with your spouse, it may be possible to get them over to your side, as it were.

However, you're changing. You're growing. You're becoming somebody else, somebody new.

Maybe they'll be excited by the prospect and decide they want to be on this journey with you.

Or maybe they won't be.

Remember, one of the ways to think about a relationship (any relationship) is in terms of a dance.

You both have set steps to follow.

When you start changing, you're no longer going to be following the regular dance steps that you used to do. You're going to start stepping on each other's toes. Your partner may insist that you change back.

Unfortunately, you're going to have to find your way out of that situation.

But, you can do it. You're an amazing artist with a unique skill set. You can do this.

Refilling the Well

I'VE MENTIONED this concept a couple of times. Basically, you have a huge well inside of yourself from which you draw inspiration and your art from.

As an artist, you need to refill this well from time to time. You may be in a situation where you already regularly do that. For me, I live on this absolutely beautiful land. My lovely husband has cut paths for me through the wilderness. A good (albeit short) hike is just outside my door. Being in nature, with all the trees and the greenery, is something that refills my well.

I do other things as well. Such as every fall, I try to make time to go and take pictures of the beautiful fall colors. I make planned trips to go to art museums. I take walks along the water. We go camping. I also spend time in the city, because I write urban fantasy and I need that city feeling as well.

So going places and viewing things is one way that I refill the well.

The other way I refill the well is by doing other art. I sometimes refer to it as my "bad art". The writing needs to be good, of a quality that other people can see it. My "bad art" is the stuff that I just do for me. A lot of my watercolor painting was bad art—just misty experiments in color.

Some of my other art isn't bad, however. I quilt. I crochet. My husband sews and makes models. He cooks—he finds that very meditative. I garden.

Much of this is art that isn't necessarily for public consumption. I don't put the pressure on myself to make it as perfect as the words.

Other writers I know refill their well by being voracious readers. They create story and they consume story. Still others refill their well by watching or listening to story.

I spend a lot of time and energy on writing, on being wildly creative. It isn't exhausting, but I do need to refill that creative well.

Check In

Pretty simple one this time. However, once you figure this out, it can profoundly change your life.

What do you do to refill your creative well?

Remember, we're growing your inner artist here. He or she needs to be fed. If you haven't been refilling your creative well, you might want to prioritize that for a while, possibly stop creating and just refill.

Asking for What You Need

MY HUSBAND WAS MUCH MORE sarcastic when I first met him, very quick with a quip. He was still incredibly supportive, but as our relationship was still new, we had to talk about what we both needed in terms of support.

Why is this important? You need people in your life who will support not only you, but who will support what you're doing in terms of your arm.

It makes all the difference in the world if you have someone on your team who's supportive of you. Not just accepting of what you do, but actively supporting it.

For example, weeks after I met my husband-to-be (not months, mere weeks) I was talking with him during an evening, and I told him what I'd managed in terms of word count for the day. I believe it was something around 3000 words, which is a nice amount of words, particularly since I still had a day job at the time.

His response? "Slacker."

I turned to him and said, "That doesn't work for me. I need you to support and celebrate my accomplishments. You can certainly tease me about my 'slacking' sometimes, but for the most part, I need you to support me. Not belittle me."

And that's been our agreement ever since. Despite how much I do accomplish, he still teases me about being a slacker. But because he supports me in everything I do, it is just gentle teasing, not a statement of how he actually feels about what I accomplish.

Check In

What do you need from your partner/spouse/best friend in terms of support?

Just saying, "I need your support" isn't good enough. Remember, they can't read your mind any more than I can. Figure out what you need, then ask them for it. If they can't give it to you, then you may end up making painful cuts. But at least you'll know why.

The Professional Side of the Equation

On Being a Professional

THIS BOOK HAS FOCUSED PRIMARILY on the artist side of things, growing your artist, becoming a more balanced and kick-ass artist, growing your confidence and shoving imposter syndrome to the curb, and so on.

However, the title of the book includes the word "professional"—as in, professional artist.

What do I mean by that?

For some definitions of the word, you become a professional once you get paid for your work. I believe that is an old-fashioned, as well as incomplete definition.

Being a professional isn't necessarily about how much money you make. Remember, making more money may or may not be in your control, and being a professional artist is all about what you, personally, *can* control.

Being a professional is about how you present yourself to the world. It's pretty simple stuff for most people, yet some artists have difficulty with it.

But it includes:

- showing up on time for a gig
- meeting deadlines
- letting your editor, manager, gallery owner, client,

whoever, know ahead of time if you are *not* going to meet a deadline
- being prepared for a gig
- meeting client expectations, or working with your client in order to come to a satisfactory compromise about what will be delivered, if possible, and if not, walking away
- having *very* clear boundaries about when you will offer your work for free or at a savings, and insisting that you get paid the rest of the time
- not shying away from contracts or negotiations
- having a work ethic

Let's break this down further.

On Time Every Time

IF YOU'RE A MUSICAL ARTIST, or a photographer, or any sort of artist who shows up for a gig, you need to get there on time. Sure, life happens. Occasionally, you may be late to something. Just make sure that life doesn't *constantly* happen to you. I know too many artists who are constantly late. That isn't professional.

As a writer, showing up on time means getting to the page as often as you can. If you are the sort of artist who has a specific writing time, get there on time. Then respect that time, be there the entire time, producing the work.

Meet Your Deadlines or Communicate

LET's talk a little about deadlines. My sweetie runs a science fiction magazine called Boundary Shock Quarterly. (http://www.boundaryshockquarterly.com). He started off with four issues, one right after another, to build interest and momentum for the project.

That meant all of the writers involved in the magazine had story deadlines the first of the month, four months in a row.

The professionals either turned in their story on time, or if they were having issues with Life or something, they communicated. They let him know *ahead of time* that they weren't going to make the deadline. Sometimes they asked for an extension. Other times they weren't in that particular issue of the magazine.

For this particular project, it really was okay if someone missed a deadline. My sweetie had built a lot of time into the schedule, so people could come in late if necessary. However, the pros communicated their issues, sometimes weeks ahead of time, so that their deadlines could be adjusted.

Be Prepared

THERE ARE a couple of aspects to this one.

One part is showing up for a gig with all the right equipment, the right camera, the right amplifier, all like that. Take the time and prepare. Make sure that you have all of the equipment ready *before* you go to the gig.

The other part involves *having* the right equipment to start with. If you're a writer, that means modern equipment and software. This doesn't mean the latest wiz-bang software and equipment. Just something that's compatible with the current market.

Let me give you an example. I know a writer who works on an ancient laptop, using a word processor that is no longer generally for sale.

Every time this writer turns something in, I end up spending thirty minutes to an hour just cleaning up the manuscript, removing all the machine code and other unreadable junk in the file. (As this writer is something of a charity case, I will do that work.) However, this writer does not meet the criteria for being a professional. If you're going to be a professional, and have electronic deliverables, you need to have the access to the correct software that's the industry standard.

Asking your editor or your client to jump through formatting hoops is, you guessed it, unprofessional.

Meeting Expectations

THIS ONE CAN BE TRICKY. As an artist, you have your internal expectations that you need to meet, in terms of your art. However, as a commercial artist, you also have client and market expectations.

If you're working individually with a client, you need to make sure that you first *set* expectations about what work is to be done, then, as a professional, you work to meet those expectations.

It's a balancing act. Sometimes your client will be delighted that you deviated from the original brief. Other times, they wanted exactly what they asked for, no more, no less.

For example, I have hired artists to do cover designs for me. For a particular book, my original concept turned out to be incorrect. What the artist came up with was so much better. (The cover in question is on the book *The Glass Magician*.)

On another, I needed an urban fantasy cover. As I tend to write between genre, and this is one series where I actually hit genre squarely, I needed a cover to convey that. While I had some beautiful cover concepts (I ran a contest on 99Designs) I couldn't choose them because I had to hit genre with the cover.

As a writer, I ignore genre and the market. I write whatever I want to write, whatever will bring me joy and make me giggle. It means that it's taken a lot longer for me to build a following.

However, once I've finished a project, I take off my writing hat, put on my marketing hat, and figure out what I need to meet market (client) expectations. What sort of cover will brand me correctly? What fonts are used by that genre? What is the pricing for that genre? And so on.

Valuing Your Work

I'VE TALKED before about valuing your work. You should get paid for what you do.

However, there I have some stories and books that I offer for free. Some of them are free for only a short time, as part of a promotion. Some of them are generally free. (I don't want to use the term perma-free, because I may change my mind and nothing is permanent.)

This work is not free because I don't value it. These stories are free because they serve as loss-leaders. Generally, the free short stories are free because they are the prequel for a longer series. At the end of that free short story there are always links to where you can read the continuing story.

Or as the joke goes, first hit's always free.

When it comes to your art, free is a tool, not a lifestyle. Embrace it as such, and wield it wisely.

Contracts

BEING a professional means not shying away from contracts. Remember, a contract is *not* for when everything goes smoothly, but for what happens when things go wrong. They are also necessary anytime money changes hands.

Let me repeat that:

A professional artist needs a contract anytime money changes hands.

This is where we go back to the last item, and up to other sections already covered as well. A professional artist values their work, and is willing to put a monetary value on it. And to not sell it/show it/play/what-have-you if that value will not be paid.

This goes along with meeting client expectations. If you've spelled out what's expected, you should also have spelled out the payment schedule, and what will be paid when.

You deserve to be paid. And if someone doesn't pay you, don't merely shrug. Send them emails. Call them. Threaten to take them to small claims court for non-payment. Start sending them registered letters.

They aren't paying you because most artists are not professionals. If you want to call yourself a professional artist, you need to act like one. Period.

Work Ethic

AS YOU CAN TELL, a lot of what it means to be a professional artist applies to your attitude.
So let's delve into the final item on the list above.
Having a work ethic.
Frequently, people comment on how much I manage to accomplish. I have a couple of friends who swear that I must have a clone who does at least half of the work, because I generally accomplish twice as much as most people.

I have no secret clone (though, believe me, there are days when I wish I did!) I don't even think of myself as being that disciplined about anything either. Quite the opposite, I consider myself fairly lazy. I am efficient, though, which is part of why I get so much done.

I also have a work ethic.
What do I mean by that?
I define myself as a writer. A writer writes. Period. She doesn't make excuses about the writing. She doesn't spend a lot of time talking about the writing. A writer writes. That's about it.

I am a fulltime writer. I don't have a regular day job. I work for myself. And believe me, I'm a much harder taskmistress than any boss you'd find out in the real world.

I was raised by two parents who worked fulltime, plus did projects around the house, plus had numerous hobbies. They were always busy. I'm like that as well. I don't own a TV though I watch shows occasionally, and I do listen to podcasts. If I am watching or listening to something, I'm also working on something else.

But mainly, I get the work done. Every single day that I can. Now, there are days when it's physically difficult or impossible to get much writing done. I can generally edit on those days. On a really bad day, I read, consume story, refill the well.

I do take time off. I play games on my phone. I try to read for pleasure, if not every night, then probably four nights out of seven. I play with my kitty, and I take time to sit on the couch and pet her, or laze bed in the morning just so she can stay next to me, curled up and purring.

Primarily, I work. Luckily, I enjoy what I do. Even when I don't, I still get it done.

And that's so much a part of what it means to be a professional artist with a work ethic. You put in the hours, butt in chair or standing behind your canvas or running scales with your instrument. Despite what anyone else thinks of you. No matter if you're recognized as an artist, if you're making your rent or merely coffee money.

Check In

FINAL CHECK in of the book! Woo and hoo for making it through!

I hope that you've spent some time thinking about yourself, your process, digging into family of origin beliefs that are holding you back, as well as processing some of the conflicting emotions you have about being an artist at a time when art and artists aren't necessarily valued.

The professional side of the equation is less about the internal and more about the external, connecting and communicating as an artist with the rest of the world.

I've given you some criterial for what I consider a professional artist should follow. Now comes the hard part.

What criteria do you think a professional artist should follow?

My list may or may not work for you. There may be additional items that I haven't thought about, that you need to add to your list. There may be items that don't work for you, or that you need to phrase differently so that they will work for you.

This time, I want you to write down your answers. Make up a physical list, whether it's in a notebook, on your computer, on your phone, just someplace.

Now, put a reminder in your calendar to revisit that list in a month's time. Possibly every month if you feel as though you're having difficulty being a professional.

Ask yourself if you're following each and every one of those criteria, if there are places where you are constantly falling down, or if could do better. Possibly you'll need to tweak the list.

This check in is *super* important.

Why?

Not because I need you to be a professional (though honestly, it will help you in every aspect of your life.) But because it's a reality check to give yourself some self-confidence.

What I hope is that you look at your list of what you need to be a professional artist every month and start saying, "Hey! I did all of those things. And I did X, Y, and Z. I guess I am a professional artist!"

I know, kind of sneaky how I added that in and brought it back to the internal trust in yourself.

As I said earlier, a lot of what it takes to be a professional artist is attitude. Call yourself a professional artist. Start acting like one. Your belief in yourself will take you further than than you realize.

You *are* a professional artist. You can do this.

Let's go.

Read More!

Be sure to pick up the other books in the Business for Breakfast series!

The Beginning Professional Writer
The Beginning Professional Publisher
The Beginning Professional Storyteller
The Intermediate Professional Storyteller
Business Planning for Professional Publishers
The Healthier Professional Writer
The Three Act Structure for Professional Writers
How to Launch a Magazine for Professional Publishers
Pulp Speed for the Professional Writer
Growing as a Professional Artist

About the Author

Leah Cutter writes page-turning fiction in exotic locations, such as a magical New Orleans, the ancient Orient, Hungary, the Oregon coast, rural Kentucky, Seattle, Minneapolis, and many others.

She writes literary, fantasy, mystery, science fiction, and horror fiction. Her short fiction has been published in magazines like *Alfred Hitchcock's Mystery Magazine* and *Talebones*, anthologies like Fiction River, and on the web. Her long fiction has been published both by New York publishers as well as small presses.

Find Leah's books here.
Follow her blog at www.LeahCutter.com.

Reviews

It's true. Reviews help me sell more books. If you've enjoyed this story, please consider leaving a review of it on your favorite site.

Come someplace new…

Are you a traveler? Do you enjoy exploring strange new worlds, new cultures, new people?

Sign up for my newsletter and I'll start you on your travels with a free copy of my book, *The Island Sampler*.

I will never spam you or use your email for nefarious purposes. You can also unsubscribe at any time.

http://www.LeahCutter.com/newsletter/

About Knotted Road Press

Knotted Road Press fiction specializes in dynamic writing set in mysterious, exotic locations.

Knotted Road Press non-fiction publishes autobiographies, business books, cookbooks, and how-to books with unique voices.

Knotted Road Press creates DRM-free ebooks as well as high-quality print books for readers around the world.

With authors in a variety of genres including literary, poetry, mystery, fantasy, and science fiction, Knotted Road Press has something for everyone.

Knotted Road Press
www.KnottedRoadPress.com

www.ingramcontent.com/pod-product-compliance
Lightning Source LLC
Chambersburg PA
CBHW070724030426
42336CB00013B/1912